CURIOSITY
The Story of NIKOLA TESLA

KENG XIONG

Published by The Child's World®
800-599-READ • www.childsworld.com

Photography Credits
Photographs ©: Napoleon Sarony/Bain News Service/George Grantham Bain Collection/Library of Congress, cover, 1, 7 (top), 8, 15; Zach Zimet/Shutterstock Images, 5; Aleksandar Todorovic/Shutterstock Images, 6; Shutterstock Images, 7 (bottom), 9, 13 (laptop), 13 (battery), 13 (outlet), 13 (light bulb), 14, 18; Stefano Bianchetti/Corbis Historical/Getty Images, 10–11; Bettmann/Getty Images, 17, 20; Design element from Napoleon Sarony/Bain News Service/George Grantham Bain Collection/Library of Congress

ISBN Information
9781503871243 (Reinforced Library Binding)
9781503872554 (Portable Document Format)
9781503873797 (Online Multi-user eBook)
9781503875036 (Electronic Publication)

LCCN 2024951063

Printed in the United States of America

Keng Xiong is an editorial assistant from Andover, Minnesota. He has a bachelor's degree in English and creative writing. In his free time, he enjoys traveling and going to bookstores.

TABLE OF CONTENTS

A CURIOUS MIND

When Nikola Tesla was a child, he saw an image of Niagara Falls. It gave him an idea for an invention. He pictured a large wheel turned by the water. His invention would use that motion to create energy people could use. Young Nikola told his uncle that one day, he would use the power of the falls.

Now it was 1896. It had taken many years. But Tesla's vision had come to life. He was ready to test it. Most electricity could be sent just 100 yards (90 m) away. But Tesla had invented a way to send energy much farther. His Niagara power plant used this new technology. With the flip of a switch, the wheel began to turn.

Waterwheels such as this one had been used to move machines for thousands of years. But Tesla's was the first to create electricity.

Tesla's invention was working! It sent electricity 20 miles (32 km) away to Buffalo, New York. Tesla's curiosity was going to change the world.

Curiosity means asking a lot of questions. These can be big or small. Curiosity includes asking *why*, *what*, and *how*. These questions help people better understand each other. This is important for forming connections.

A statue honoring Tesla and his power plant stands near Niagara Falls.

Asking questions can also help people learn about complex topics. Tesla worked with electricity. It is very complex. He needed curiosity to learn about it and try new things.

Tesla used his curiosity to create new solutions. But first, he had to learn more about the world around him. He would need to look for answers to problems. He stayed curious and open to new ideas. His studies and work would later help him come up with his own inventions.

In 1897, Tesla gave a speech celebrating the success of his power plant. Tesla talked to the crowd about his ideas:

> *"With ideas it is like with dizzy heights you climb: At first they cause you discomfort and you are anxious to get down, distrustful of your own powers; but soon the remoteness of the* ***turmoil*** *of life and the inspiring* ***influence*** *of the* ***altitude*** *calm your blood; your step gets firm and sure and you begin to look—for dizzier heights."*

Source: "Tesla's 'Power Banquet' Speech." *Tesla Science Center at Wardenclyffe*, January 12, 2019. http://teslasciencecenter.org.

THE VALUE OF CURIOSITY

Nikola Tesla was born on July 10, 1856. He grew up in the Austrian Empire, now Croatia. Growing up, Tesla was always curious. He could be found in his father's library. He did well in his schoolwork. Tesla enjoyed math and science. He could solve difficult math problems in his head. His teachers were impressed. Some thought he was cheating. But Tesla was not.

I had three sisters and a brother.

People can visit a memorial center at Tesla's birth home in Croatia.

Tesla came up with all kinds of interesting inventions, including neon lights, remote control, and the magnifying transmitter (pictured).

Tesla was creative and imaginative. Throughout his studies, he learned about inventions. He studied engineering in college. He learned about new topics such as **physics**. He also learned about electricity. Tesla asked his professors many questions. He always wanted to learn more.

The more Tesla learned, the more he wanted to work on his own ideas. Tesla's curiosity motivated him. He began creating inventions. In 1884, Tesla left his home. He **immigrated** to the United States to pursue greater dreams and questions.

Tesla was especially curious about electricity. At that time, most people used direct current (DC) electricity. With DC, the **electrons** flow in one direction. DC was easy to work with. But it was difficult to send this electricity long distances.

Scientists had developed early versions of alternating current (AC) electricity. With AC, the electrons quickly change directions. AC was better for sending electricity long distances. But it was also more difficult to use. Tesla wanted to improve AC electricity. He had to ask questions and brainstorm new ideas. Then he had to do experiments.

DIRECT CURRENT VERSUS ALTERNATING CURRENT

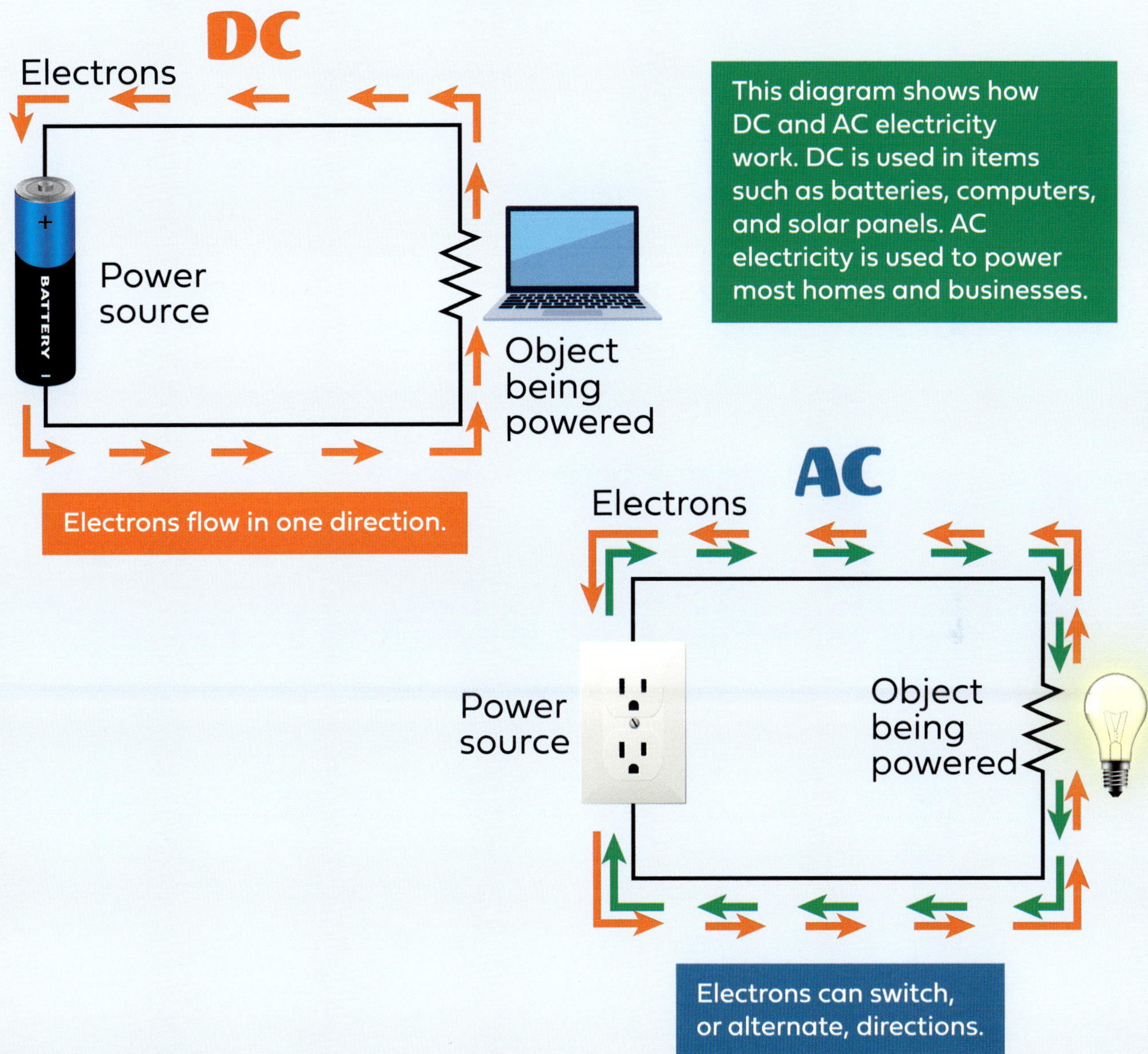

This diagram shows how DC and AC electricity work. DC is used in items such as batteries, computers, and solar panels. AC electricity is used to power most homes and businesses.

THOMAS EDISON

Tesla arrived in the United States in 1884. He began working for Thomas Edison. But they did not see things the same way. Edison focused on **marketing** inventions to the public. That did not interest Tesla. He wanted to create his own ideas. Tesla also did not think he was being paid enough. Less than a year after meeting, Tesla parted ways with Edison.

Thomas Edison supported DC. Tesla supported AC. The 1893 Chicago world's fair used AC in its demonstrations. This helped Tesla's system win what became known as the War of the Currents.

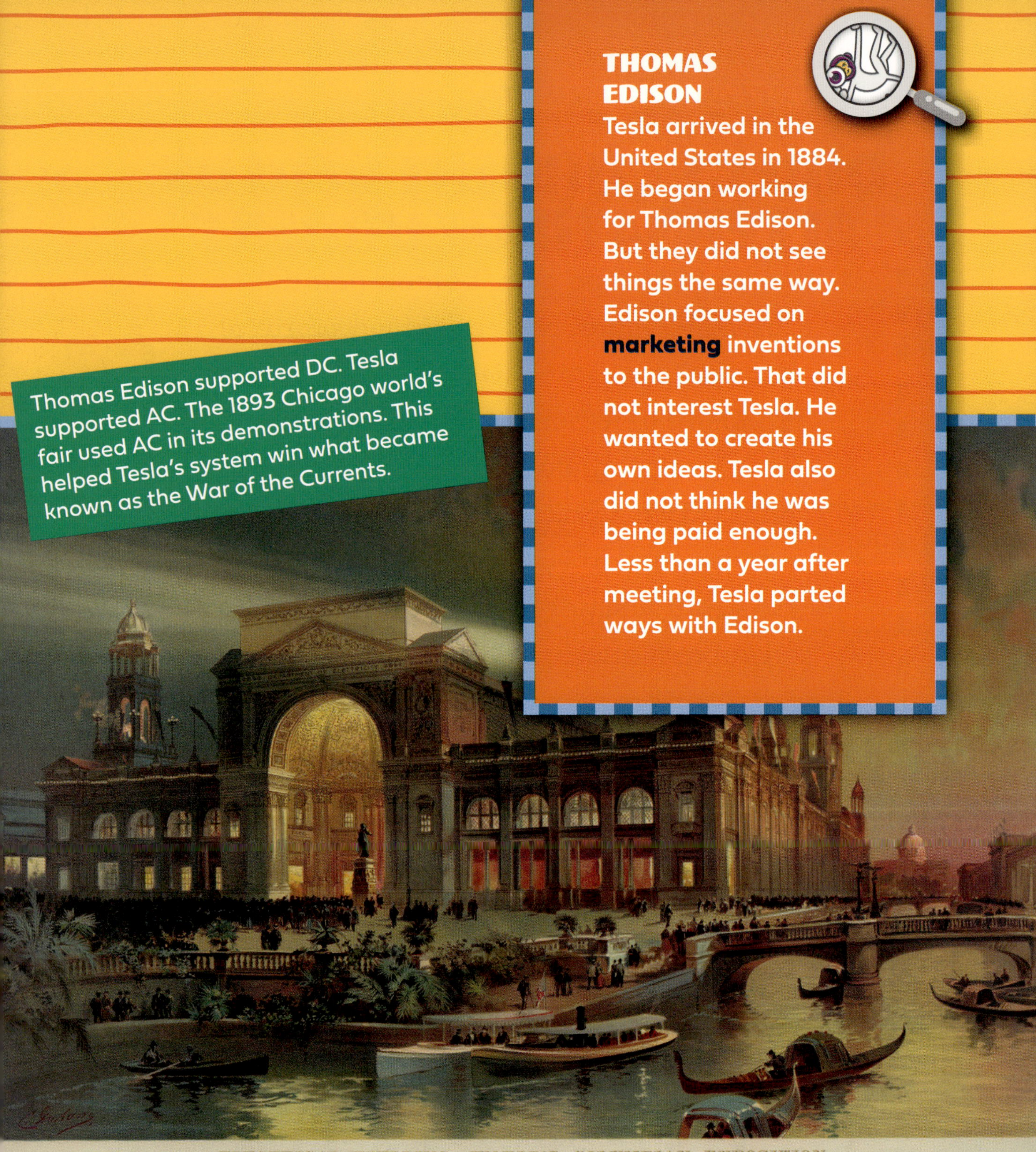

ELECTRICAL BUILDING—WORLD'S COLUMBIAN EXPOSITION.

Around 1887, Tesla found a way to make AC work well. He started making AC motors. These were more powerful than DC motors. They also had the ability to send electricity much farther. This meant more people could have access to electricity. Today, AC powers many devices and technologies. All it took was a curious spark.

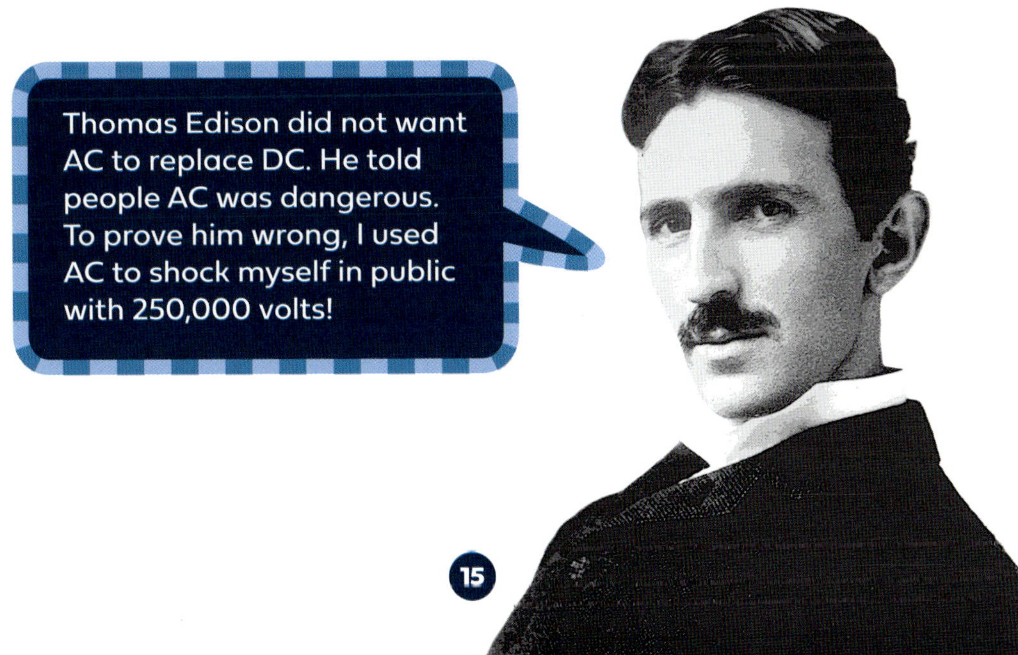

CREATIVE POSSIBILITIES

Curiosity leads to new ways of thinking. In 1891, Tesla brainstormed a new idea. He imagined a device with a large metal coil. It would be able to power other devices using electricity. He called it the Tesla coil. He imagined Tesla coils set up all over Earth. They would create large amounts of electricity for people to use. They would also allow electricity to travel through the air. This meant electricity would not need a **conductor**. Tesla hoped devices would get power just by being near a coil. Electricity would not need wires.

Tesla learned that he could send radio waves through the Tesla coil. This discovery led to the invention of the radio.

TESLA, INC.

In 2003, Martin Eberhard and Marc Tarpenning founded a new company. They wanted to create high-quality electric cars. The founders called their company Tesla Motors in honor of Nikola Tesla. Today, Tesla, Inc. focuses on **sustainable** energy. It makes batteries and solar panels. Tesla is also one of the most popular electric car brands.

Visitors to the Nikola Tesla Museum in Belgrade, Serbia, can see a Tesla coil in action. The coil wirelessly powers lights held by visitors.

The invention was a big idea. It would require materials and money. Tesla created working coils. But his dream of coils around the world did not come true. Still, Tesla's idea inspired curiosity in others.

Over time, people built on Tesla's idea. Today there are many types of wireless technology. People can use wireless headphones. Cell phones can be charged wirelessly. And the internet connects people around the world. These technologies came from Tesla's coil idea.

Tesla in 1933

Tesla died on January 7, 1943. But his influence can still be seen today. Tesla's inventions helped improve the power of electricity. His curiosity never ended. It helped change the world.

WONDER MORE

Wondering About New Information

How much did you know about curiosity and Nikola Tesla before reading this book? What new information did you learn? Write down three new facts that this book taught you. Was the new information surprising? Why or why not?

Wondering How It Matters

What is one way that curiosity relates to your life? Is there anything you are curious about? What are your friends curious about? Do you know any other curious people?

Wondering Why

Being curious requires asking questions. Tesla put his curiosity to work in finding solutions to everyday problems. Why is it important to ask questions before starting on a solution? What do you have to consider before starting?

Ways to Keep Wondering

Curiosity is a complex topic. After reading this book, what questions do you have about it? What can you do to learn more about being curious?

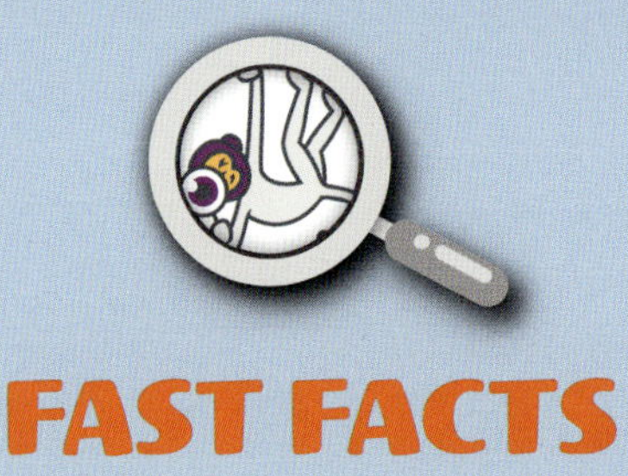

FAST FACTS

- Curiosity helps people understand the world. Asking questions is one way to stay curious.
- Nikola Tesla was born on July 10, 1856. He grew up in what is now Croatia. He was interested in learning more about science.
- Tesla showed curiosity when thinking of new ideas and inventions. He also showed curiosity even when his inventions did not work.
- Tesla died on January 7, 1943. His inventions, such as the Tesla coil, have made a great impact on today's world.

ASKING CURIOUS QUESTIONS

1. Put your own curiosity to the test. Brainstorm a new invention that could improve your everyday life. It could be big or small. Why is this invention needed? Who do you need help from? What questions might you ask?
2. Draw it out! What does this solution look like? What materials do you need?
3. Share your invention with someone. What do they notice about your invention? Do they have feedback about how to improve it?

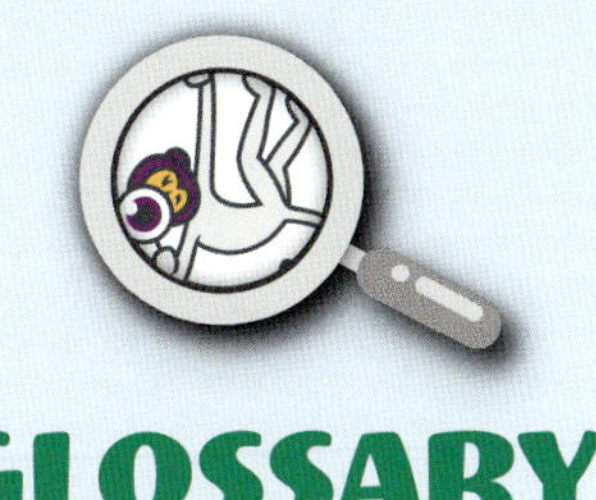

GLOSSARY

altitude (AL-tih-tood) Altitude is the vertical distance of something, such as a mountain's height above sea level. Tesla compared following his ideas to climbing to a high altitude on a mountain.

conductor (kun-DUK-ter) A conductor is a material that electricity can flow through, such as steel or brass. Tesla coils do not need a conductor to create electricity.

electrons (ee-LEK-tronz) Electrons are particles, or tiny parts of something, charged with electricity. Alternating current lets electrons change direction.

immigrated (IH-muh-gray-ted) Someone who immigrated has moved from their home country to a different country. Tesla immigrated to the United States.

influence (IN-floo-inss) An influence is something that affects others. Tesla was an influence to many inventors.

marketing (MAR-keh-ting) Marketing is showcasing or selling a product. Thomas Edison focused on marketing his inventions to the public.

physics (FIH-ziks) Physics is a science that focuses on how energy affects things that take up space and have weight. Tesla took classes about physics.

sustainable (suh-STAY-nuh-bull) Something sustainable uses a resource without damaging it. Tesla, Inc. works on sustainable energy sources, such as solar panels.

turmoil (TUR-moyl) Turmoil is a state of confusion, disturbance, and restlessness. Tesla used his ideas as a way to escape the turmoil of life.

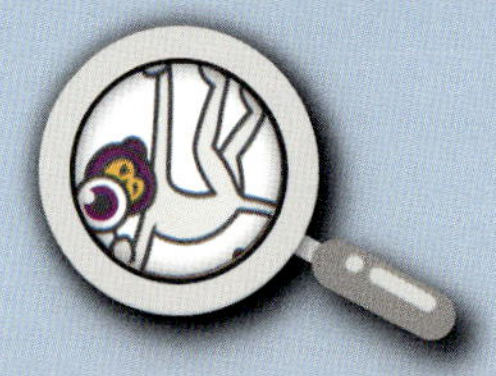

FIND OUT MORE

In the Library

Oldfield, Molly. *Everything Under the Sun: A Curious Question for Every Day of the Year.* Tulsa, OK: Kane Miller, 2022.

Sherman, Suzanne. *The Shocking Story of Electricity.* New York, NY: DK Publishing, 2023.

Xiong, Keng. *Determination: The Story of Thomas Edison.* Parker, CO: The Child's World, 2026.

On the Web

Visit our website for links about curiosity and Nikola Tesla:
childsworld.com/links

Note to Parents, Caregivers, Teachers, and Librarians: We routinely verify our web links to make sure they are safe and active sites. So encourage your readers to check them out!

INDEX